TABLE OF CONTENTS

How To Create, Market & Sell Videobooks
Every Author Should Get In On This Amazing Book
Format!
©Copyright 2014 by Dr. Treat Preston

DISCLAIMER AND TERMS OF USE AGREEMENT:

(Please Read This Before Using This Book)

This information is for educational and informational purposes only. The content is not intended to be a substitute for any professional advice, diagnosis, or treatment.

The authors and publisher of this book and the accompanying materials have used their best efforts in preparing this book.

The authors and publisher make no representation or warranties with respect to the accuracy, applicability, fitness, or completeness of the contents of this book. The information contained in this book is strictly for educational purposes. Therefore, if you wish to apply

Introduction – Videobooks Is A New Reading Experience

As an author, I am constantly on the lookout for new ideas, new formats, new marketing techniques, and new ways to get the word out. I learned very early in my writing career that writing the actual book was the easy part; marketing and selling the book was the difficult part.

In the past, I used mainstream publishers that contracted to do the marketing and selling but they left me wanting; they just didn't do the job. Then I was introduced to ePubWealth.com, which is a full service publishing house but also has a self indie publishing arm and I finally found what I had been seeking my entire writing career. ePubWealth.com allows me to pick and choose whatever I want in marketing and promotion and I like that.

It is at ePubWealth where I learned about videobooks and after I published my first one, I absolutely went nuts about the concept. My videobooks quickly outpaced all of my other book formatted sales and I began to study the metrics closely.

The concept of videobooks is not new but using video as a publishing format for a good many types of genres is new. When you think of it for just a moment, it makes sense. The viewing public prefers video and audio over any printed format just like they do in the main internet world.

The videobook format is not for any and all genres and I will discuss this in detail in Chapter 4. I will also give you resources in creating and producing videobooks but also what platforms you can place them on for maximum sales.

Next, since videobooks are visual, illustrating your books is very important but I will show you how to NOT overdo the illustration aspect. Videobooks are NOT movies! Okay, let's get to the good stuff now...

Chapter 1 – What is a Videobook?

Defining what a videobook is can be tricky mainly because everyone has their preconceived notion of what a videobook is and generally it is wrong.

Here is an example of how even Wikipedia gets it wrong.

Videobook
http://en.wikipedia.org/wiki/Videobook

VideoBook is a brand of online, interactive educational videos marketed by Studio 21.

History

The name "Videobook" was first registered and used in the United Kingdom (UK) in 1982 by Mr. Barry R. Pyat, who was then the owner of Yorkshire film producers

"Studio 21." Video Book was the marquee, trading title, and style for an innovative set of local-interest and sell-through video films. The name Video Book was in commercial use by Studio 21 in the UK and Spain until 2003. In 2004, Mr. Pyat opened Angel Films in Spain, which took over the Video Book marquee. In 2005, Angel Films UK was established, and in 2008, Video Book products were re-launched in the UK. All of the Video Books are identified and registered with the ISBN agencies. The trademark style is as one word, with uppercase V and uppercase B, in a modified Bookman typeface, and are the exclusive property of Mr. B. Pyatt, and have been in continuous commercial use since 1982.

The name "videobook" (without the two uppercase characters) has also become a standard term for a form of online training that delivers web-based training via downloadable training videos. Most video books are single website entities that focus on teaching the user (typically a subscriber) a particular topic (see links below for examples). Video books are, as the name implies, similar in content and outline to a "regular" book. The videos are typically recorded by a trained instructor and offered to the viewer on a subscription-based model. The user visits the video book (the website containing the training videos), purchases a subscription, and can then download any or all of the training videos.

Videobooks are different from many Computer-based training (C.B.T) models in that video book videos are typically in a shareable and portable format. They also differ in the content delivery.

The basic component of a videobook is video, compared to a printed book or an audio book, which rely solely on text or audio, respectively. The video book can have on-screen text along with pictures and video clips, if necessary. The text displayed may get animated along with related audio commentary in the background.

- Delivery: typically, web-based delivery in video format; downloadable videos, free of cost or at low cost for a subscription
- Focus: teaching a specific task (task-based videos)
- Student freedom: the student can watch the videos in any order they wish; the videos are presented in a recommended order but, due to the downloadable model, students can download and watch videos in any sequence.
- Teacher freedom: Videobooks provide freedom to expert to prepare video content in the way he/she wants.
- Connectivity: requires no Internet connection to watch the video (Internet connection is required to download the video however)
- Portability: the videos are portable and use non-proprietary video formats—users can watch the video on any computer and most portable devices
- Target group: target market is usually the individual instead of a corporation or company department
- Cost of preparation: Videobooks are very cost-effective and easy to develop using low cost screen capturing software.
- Process of preparation: Videobooks may be prepared for any topic using a) presentation

software such as PowerPoint, b) screen capturing software such as Camtasia and c) Text-to-Speech software, such as TextAloudMP3 to provide audio commentary. With the use of these three powerful tools any expert can develop videobooks at his leisure time, modify and finetune the content as per student feedback and release improved versions of videobooks conveniently. Readers who are interested in developing videobooks on their own are requested to browse http://one-task-at-a-time.tripod.com to learn step-by-step procedures to develop videobooks.

Competition and comparison

Videobooks often get lumped in with CBTs (Computer-based training) and e-learning categories, yet they are distinctly different. A comparative analysis of each is listed below:

Computer-based training (CBT) is a very effective medium for training employees. Although it offers an excellent ROI, CBTs often carry a high start-up cost for business looking to realize and are therefore marketed mostly to companies/departments (cost is often too high for an individual to purchase). CBTs are an excellent tool for training and can feature online (trackable) quizzes, excellent examples and 3D motion video. Many CBTs can be viewed offline (no connection to the Internet may ever be required) and most CBTs are delivered via CD-ROM or DVD via postal mail or in-store purchase. CBTs are historically proprietary and often require special software to be installed on the user's computer.

E-learning and videobooks are also often compared because both models use the web for content delivery. The main differences between the two are cost (e-learning is typically not a low-cost medium), target market (e-learning has historically been too costly for individuals and so the target market has primarily been companies and departments), and portability (e-learning requires an Internet connection to participate).

*****

Now, Wikipedia is not stating anything that is untrue; it is just that videobooks has moved on and have progressed way past the point of the Wikipedia article. Yes, videobooks are still a very viable format for training and education but today they are so much more.

To the point – a videobook is taking an existing book of content and combining an audiobook format of narration with illustrations where a viewer can listen and participate in the book's content as the book is read aloud and the illustrations are viewed.

Here is an example of a children's videobook:

http://youtu.be/iYA4CXgn1fA

In the case of many videobooks, the viewer really enjoys the format because with videobooks, it is both entertaining and informative and now encompasses so many different genres.

Now think for just a moment of the advantages that videobooks bring to the table:

- In lieu of PowerPoint presentations and using a book as the content, creating a videobook is a better format and actually reaches more viewers.

- In actuality, if authors pay close attention to how they illustrate their books and videobooks, in essence the author is creating a mini-movie where the printed word is augmented with a visual message too. This is very powerful in capturing viewers.

- Quality production is essential. Using the best graphic artists to do the illustrations and the best narrators to do the audio is so very important in order to produce the best product. Making sure that the illustrations match the storyline and are in the proper place in the narration almost guarantees success.

- As with any printed book, conducting proper research that demonstrates what readers/viewers are looking for determines the quantity of sales. For example, producing a printed book or videobook on the "mating habits of amoebas" just doesn't cut it with readers/viewers. They want topics that entertain, teach or both.

- By design, videobooks can be viewed easily on any desktop, laptop, tablet or cell phone. It is extremely portable and an easy format to store to use at any time

- In the past, authors considered videobooks for existing books they have written but now, authors are considering books that are especially viable for the videobook format.

- In cases of budgetary considerations, videobooks can easily be produced using software such as Camtasia with the author as the narrator. Skilled graphic designers, such as the ones I have listed in the resource section, can be engaged at affordable prices to do the illustrations.

Now let's move on to the next chapter and discuss how to create videobooks...

Chapter 2 – How to Create a Videobook

Creating a videobook is more than just creating a video. Like I stated previously, in essence you are creating a mini-movie but it is more detailed and the length of videobook is not as important as it is in movie production.

Here are the components of a videobook production:

1. **Script/Content** – An existing book's written content is NOT the script. Yes, the narrator will be reading the book's content word-for-word but laying out the book's content to be narrator is placing it in script format so that the narrator gets it right.

Graphics – My graphic designer completes all of my illustrations and graphic content in advance and I have her place all of them within the narrative before I begin production. Also make sure you do a DVD Album cover for your book.

DVD Album Requirements:
Cover jpeg 1448 x 1448 pixels

2. **Production** – When I do it myself I use Camtasia (see resource section) and place the content in a plain PowerPoint background complete with illustrations. The graphic designer I recommend in the resource section – Sanchita Dutta – can do this for you along with the illustrations.

TIP: Sanchita does all of my illustrations and I also include these illustrations in my print versions of the book.

If you are producing the videobook yourself as narrator then use a service like Cueprompter: http://www.cueprompter.com/ to assist you. I use Cueprompter when I produce my own videobooks and I like it a lot.

If you are doing the narration part and using recording software like Audacity (see resource section) then set your recording to the following settings:

Constant bitrate
44.1 KHz
16-bit
2-channel stereo files
320Bps
Lame dll file

TIP: If you used Camtasia, then you do not need to set any settings. Camtasia does the visual as well as audio. Only use Audacity to separately record the audio and then marry it to the video using post production editing software.

3. **Post-Production** – this is the editing phase and unless you know how to edit then please allow a professional editor to do it. You can find professional editors at any video production house. Just look in your local Yellow Pages.

4. **Optional techniques that work!**

What I have discovered is that by placing advertising inside the videobook allows the viewers to access more of your "stuff".

ALWAYS place the advertising at the end of the videobook. NEVER place it at the beginning or within the videobook content.

There are different offers that you can use. I have used all of the following with great success:

Free Offer – I always provide a free offer for my viewers. The one that I use that is most effective is at the end of this book:

Remember, never use more than two offers per videobook!!! Furthermore, you cannot expect a viewer to remember a sales page URL: to

Amazon or CreateSpace so pick a really good
domain URL that they can remember.

Example: For the book "How To Retire Without
Money" I used the URL
http://www.RetireWithoytMoney.org. Viewers
had no problem remembering this URL. Click on
the link and check out the sales page.

Next, you can offer a packaged product. I have 8-
survival books that I offer at a deep discount
price. Package them all in one download at a
package price

Okay, now let's discuss how to market your videobook…

Chapter 3 – How to Market & Sell Videobooks

I have a saying that I use all of the time, "Nothing happens until you sell something!" and the sale does not stop with the exchange of money. Customer service is always important and responding promptly to any customer requests is of the utmost importance.

Next, whenever possible, capture your customer's contact info in an autoresponder where you can make additional promo offers to them, giveaway free stuff, and just stay in touch. I use AWeber as my autoresponder system:

http://www.aweber.com/?284935

Don't you just love that word FREE?

Authors spend gobs of money on book promotions and I am going to show you "How to Create and Promote Viral Video Book Trailers" and best of all it is all FREE!

Video rocks and you can drive a good deal of traffic to your book sites using video trailers.

It is much easier for your videos to get ranked high and with the methods you are going to learn, you'll be easily able to dominate even the most competitive terms.

According to a recent article in TechCrunch, Youtube is currently serving about 1.2 Billion videos per day and more than 200,000 new videos are being uploaded every day. With Youtube videos collectively receiving billions of views per day, the opportunity for us, the marketers is IMMENSE.

According to Quantcast, Youtube reaches to over 122 million US people monthly (Global figures are much higher) and only Google and Facebook have slightly higher reach than this amazing platform.

Youtube recently replaced Yahoo! As the no.2 search engine, meaning more and more people are using it for finding information and doing research. It's no longer just an entertainment site.

According to a study by Clickstream, there has been an increase of over 300% in the number of people leaving search engines and going to video sharing sites, which shows that people are now more than ever inclined to leave text based sites to video oriented sites.

Actually this shift was long expected.....It's a proven fact that most of the people prefer watching video than reading through lengthy text. Now the decreased cost of hosting, advancement in web technology and faster than ever internet connections have allowed a large section of both the internet marketers and general internet users to share and consume information in the video format.

Most of the internet marketers are still either plain ignorant about the potential of this massive traffic channel or don't know how to tap on its user base.

I am not exaggerating but it's a matter of fact: If the past decade belonged to PPC and Article marketing then the next one is going to belong to video marketing.

Youtube and other video sharing sites have enabled us (The ordinary individuals) to spread our message (be it political, religious, business related or just for fun) to a wide audience. Until a few years ago, this privilege was reserved for the major television networks and their wealthy advertisers. For many businesses (small enterprises as well as Fortune500 companies), Youtube has become the main promotional platform. There is a friend of mine who has developed a big six figure IM business out of the Youtube alone.

This book should be used in conjunction with the book. "How to Promote Your Book Online and Offline," http://www.amazon.com/dp/B00AS7PDCK and is one of the many sequel books to this main promotional book.

It is part of my ePublishing series of books:

*Author Blueprint
http://www.amazon.com/dp/B00G00HYK8
*Copyright Law Guidebook
http://www.amazon.com/dpB00BHEYBK8
*Distraction Video Marketing
http://www.amazon.com/dp/B00BURDLAI
*How To Create, Market & Sell Audiobooks
http://www.amazon.com/dp/B00BQZXBZE
How to Get FREE Publicity and Interviews
http://www.amazon.com/dp/B00CNTJAQ6
*How to Promote Your Book Online & Offline Vol 1
http://www.amazon.com/dp/B00AS7PDCK
*How To Promote Your Book Online & Offline Vol 2
http://www.amazon.com/dp/B00BDTEILO
*How To Promote Your Book Online & Offline Vol 3
http://www.amazon.com/dp/B00C42T2JC

*How to Write a Kindle Book in Hours
http://www.amazon.com/dp/B008XOY8VC
*How to Write Compelling Content
http://www.amazon.com/dp/B00B5QWYTI
*International Standard Book Numbers
http://www.amazon.com/dp/B00B2YB4SK
*Promoting Your Video Book Trailers
http://www.amazon.com/dp/B00BCDHEMG
*Publish with a Purpose
http://www.amazon.com/dp/B008Z5U4LC
*Star Power - Using Celebrities for Interviews & Promotions
http://www.amazon.com/dp/B00CJSWN6K
*The Overwhelmed Author
http://www.amazon.com/dp/B00CBI3XA8
*The ePubWealth Program
http://www.amazon.com/dp/B008HHHVO6
*The ePubWealth Program ADVANCED
http://www.amazon.com/dp/B00B65PGCA
*The Publishing Agreement
http://www.amazon.com/dp/B00BKGTQZI
*Viral Image Marketing
http://www.amazon.com/dp/B00C4MFGJ2

As I teach you video marketing I need you to remember these words – consistency, diversity and relevant content, and notice these three things are the same as in backlinking and article marketing.

In today's world of search engine marketing (SEM) these three things are what ALL of the search engines are looking for and demanding otherwise they literally ignore your stuff and all of your efforts are wasted.

21

Not good!

Video marketing is one of the most important promo techniques an author has available to them and only backlinking is more important. Video marketing is inexpensive and literally quite easy to do. So let's get at it…

First, I want to introduce you to some of my most famous or infamous rants…

"Nothing happens until you sell something!" – When people ask me what I do for a living I respond by telling them I am a salesman. I have two doctorate degrees and 10-years of college so they usually say something like this: "Why would you tell people you are a salesman when you are a doctor? A doctor is more prestigious than a salesman."

People, you can "STICK" prestige in your back pocket. Sales have made me a healthier income than at any time as a doctor when I was practicing. I am in business to make a living and not impress anybody. As an author, you use your talents to create excellent relevant content and without authors the world would be ignorant.

Unfortunately, many creative types of people like authors have virtually no ability to market and promote their work and unless people see it and read it then it quickly becomes an exercise in futility.

You have to sell it!

"The meaning of words is not in the words; they are in us!" – In the book, "How To Write Compelling Content," http://www.amazon.com/dp/B00B5QWYTI, I describe in detail that the conscious mind sees reality for what it is but the subconscious mind "perceives" this reality and the perception can be different than the reality itself.

In other words, reality means nothing; perception is everything.

And since all behavior/conduct/actio0n stems from the subconscious mind, an author's goal should always be to "capture" the subconscious mind.

Your capture a person's "attention" by your book cover, book description and overt ad tactics but you capture their minds with your content and the meaning of the words you write are not in the words, they are in your readers as they "perceive" them.

23

"Hunting is for fools who have never heard about bait!" – You don't hunt for customers! You bait them! And I am not talking "bait and switch" here; don't even go there. You bait them with a great product and a great price and fantastic support.

But to begin, your content has to be relevant and entertaining and this is why video rocks!

People would rather watch a video than read so your video should be designed to capture FIRST their attention and then your content captures their mind!

"Doing your best is the devil's lie; I need you to do what is REQUIRED!" – When I was growing up, my father who was a building contractor would assigned me tasks to do daily.

Woe was me if I ever used the words, "Dad, I did the best I could," because I would soon find myself lying on my back spitting teeth.

His response was, "I didn't tell you to do your best; I told you to do what is required."

Doin your best is the devil's lie. It gives you an excuse to blame and blame is a totally useless concept. When it comes right down to it; you only have choices in life not excuses.

Here is my point: what I teach you in this book is completely worthless unless you follow my instruction and make the Mojo happen by doing what is REQUIRED.

"Many people know the price of everything but the value of nothing." – Never in the history of mankind has there been a more accurate statement than this one. You may know the price of everything but value is mutually exclusive from price.

Let me give you an example – everyone knows the price of a Rolls Royce motor car is astronomical but it is a very exclusive car and expensive because it is mostly handmade.

What if I told you that you could own this car for just $50/month?

Everybody would rush out and get one and the value of the car would decline because it is no longer exclusive.

In this example, debt service is more important than price.

In fact, no one care what the price of anything is as long as they can make small monthly payments and enjoy the product. Car leasing is another example of this fact!

"You cannot trust dogs to watch your food." – Go with me on this one…enough said!

Opportunity Knocks

Opportunity Knocks and most often many of you aren't paying attention!!

In publishing, an author can never let any marketing and promotional technique get past them. Recently, one of my author associates came up with a program that is simply neat.

He has been toying around with video and has produced some great stuff. Go see: http://youtu.be/IRuC_X53uAI

He built this video using GoAnimate and Sparkol. Then he posts the video on Gumroad (see resource section).

This is how Gumroad works and it is taken directly from their website…

Features

- **Sell where you share**

  Sell to your fans, friends, and followers in the same ways that you communicate with them.

- **Stick to creating**

  Continuously create cool stuff, while all of your hosting, delivery, and payment needs are taken care of by Gumroad.

- **Fast and secure**

We securely encrypt and expire every file hosted on Gumroad, generated uniquely at time-of-sale for each purchase. Best part: honest users will never even notice.

- **As simple as sharing a link**

No store needed. Want to sell just one track? Gumroad lets you do that. No need to set things up that you don't need.

- **Talk directly to your customers**

Gumroad lets you talk directly with your customers. So that you can send them a thank you note, or ping them with an update to something they bought previously.

- **Frictionless payments**

Gumroad has the best buying experience on the web. Really. Don't believe that? See it in action here.
Long gone are the days of filling out shipping information to buy... an MP3.

- **Automatic delivery**

Once a payment has gone through, Gumroad instantly emails your new customer with a fast, secure download link.

- **Collect shipping information**

If you want to sell a physical album, T-shirt, or even send them a thank you note in the mail, you can enable the collection of shipping information for your buyers.

- **Choose your own pricing**

   You deserve the ability to dynamically price your creations. With pay-what-you-want pricing, you can let your customers decide what they think your stuff is worth to them!

- **Built-in previews**

   Have a preview image? Upload it and showcase it alongside your content. Have a 30 second audio clipping? That works too.

The best part of Gumroad is that there are no redirects away from the Facebook site.

How To Make Simple Videos By Using A Webcam

There are basically two ways to record a video using your webcam. With Youtube: You'll need two things to record a video with Youtube and your webcam:

*A Youtube Account

*A webcam installed in your computer. Most of the new computers come with a webcam installed.

Now follow the steps below to record and upload your videos:

Login to your Youtube account. Once you are in, you'll see a link named "upload" in the top, click on that.

Next you'll see a link named "Record from your webcam", click on that.

Next you'll see something like this:

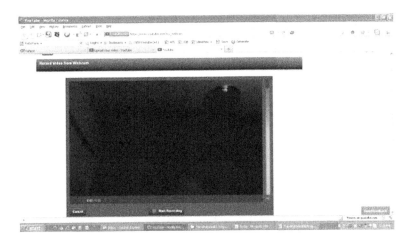

In the "privacy" settings, you'll need to allow it to access your camera and microphone.

Hit the close button in the pop-up. Now you should see your picture (if you are sitting in from of your computer), if not then you'll need to choose a different video source from the video drop down in the "record video" window.

Once you see your picture, hit the "record" button.

Once you finish recording, click on the "done" button if you are satisfied with the quality or hit the "re-record" to record it again. After you hit the "done" button, your video will be automatically uploaded to Youtube and start processing. You can edit the information anytime by clicking on the "My Videos" link (http://Youtube.com/my_videos) If have problem in using your webcam, be sure to check if your firewall settings are not blocking the connection to your server.

31

Once your video is uploaded and processed, you can download it with the help of "Download Helper" plugin. This plugin works seamlessly with Firefox and allows you to download videos in different format and different screen sizes. You can download this plugin from the link below:

http://DownloadHelper.net

After downloading, you can submit it to other video sites like Metacafe, Dailymotion, Google Video, Vimeo etc with the help of TubeMogul or HeySpread.

Video Marketing Blueprint

Video Marketing

A Simple 3 Step Process for Uncovering Profitable Keywords

1. Find 5 keywords with 3,000+ searches/month

2. Look for keywords that have no more than 30,000 competing video results on YouTube

3. Look for keywords with less than 20,000 "keyword" competitors on Google (search with quotes).

These are just guidelines to use. You can target if a few of the videos in the top 5 have less than 10,000 views don't just instantly dismiss the keyword. Maybe the existing videos just aren't very good. If you know it's a keyword that works well in Google, use it on YouTube.

If you already have a product, then you probably already know a few keywords that you'd like to rank high for on YouTube.

How to Get Your Video Ranked on the 1st Page of YouTube

If you want to get more traffic, optins and sales then you need to learn how to get your videos ranked at the top of YouTube. Although YouTube is owned by Google, they have their own unique algorithm for ranking videos. However, there are a few similarities. Video SEO is very similar to SEO in that there is…

1) On-Page Optimization

2) Off-Page Optimization

Good on-page optimization is one of the most critical factors of success in getting high rankings on both

Google and YouTube so we're going to start with on-page optimization first.

How to Optimize Your Videos to Rank High on YouTube

Use the keyword you want to rank in the video title

Make sure your keyword is also in the description box

Put your keyword in the tags, along with any other related keywords that you want to rank

Here's a screenshot of what a well optimized video should look like.

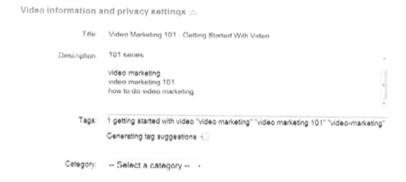

Here are 3 main keywords this video is trying to rank:

"Video Marketing" "Video Marketing 101" "Getting Started with Video

As you can see, they are all in the title box, the description box and the tag box (though you don't see them all in the tags in this screenshot)

Here are some more general guidelines to follow:

☐ Only focus on 1 or 2 keywords per video and don't try to rank a video for more than 2 or 3 keywords.

It's better to narrow in on one or two keywords and be perfectly optimized for them than it is to try to rank 3-4 different keywords with 1 video and miss them all because you were trying to hit them all with 1 swing.

☐ Always make sure you put the full title in the tags and each of the individual keywords as well.

☐ Put your keywords in quotes in the tags, it helps.

☐ Put your keywords in the description box too.

The #1 Biggest Mistake Most People Make When Tagging Their Videos

They don't put their URL in the beginning of the description box!

I can't even begin to tell you how many videos I see that have their URL buried deep in their description where you can't even see it!

When you're watching a video on YouTube, the only thing you can see is the first line of the description box.

So if your URL is not in the first line, people won't see it!

And if they don't see it, they won't click on it and you won't get any traffic or leads (which is the whole point of everything we've been talking about!)

Fact is people are lazy and over 90% will never open your description box to see what you wrote in it. In fact, most people probably won't even watch your video until the end.

Make sure you make it easy for people to click on your link by ALWAYS putting it in the very beginning of the description box like this….

http://www.YourWebsiteHere.com

Note: if you don't put the http in front, it won't be clickable. That's another huge mistake that a lot of people make.

I know this all sounds really basic but I see so many people screw it up that I purposely decided to make this its own separate section in order to drill it into you!

Also, make sure you capitalize your URL exactly like I showed you. It looks better and gets more people to click.

How to Get YouTube to Do All the Hard Work for You and Get Tons of Views on Auto-Pilot

Here's another really neat trick that'll help you get tons of views fast

1) Find the top 5 videos in your niche or for your keyword

2) Pull up their video and look at their tags

3) Copy and paste the tags they're using into your tags

I know this sounds really simple but it's extremely powerful.

Not only will this help you rank on YouTube for the same keywords they're targeting but it'll also get your video featured on the sidebar where it shows the related videos.

What YouTube does is it "sniffs out" related videos based on the keyword relevancy in the titles, tags, and description etc.

So if you're optimized the same as the most popular videos, you have a much better chance of having your video featured to the right.

It's basically like having PPC/Banner Ads featured on the sidebar of one the most popular websites in your niche.

Except it's totally free!

This is probably my favorite part about YouTube.

If you tag your videos right, they basically do the promotion FOR you. They feature your videos on the sidebar of other related videos and you get tons of views from people that are clicking around on all the related videos and watching video after video.

I don't know about you but I'm kind of lazy so the idea of optimizing my video correctly and getting views right away without having to build any links is pretty sweet. That'll never happen with SEO.

How to Get More People to Watch Your Videos

Okay, so your videos optimized correctly but you may not be getting ranked on the first page quite yet. However, you're probably getting views from being listed in the related videos section if you applied the tips I just shared.

Now the question to ask is: How can I get more people to click my videos?

Well, you can think of your featured video as a banner ad because it's basically just a headline and a picture.

And since those are the 2 main things that determine click-thru rates with banner ads, the same principles apply here.

2 Tips to Capture People's Attention and Get them to Watch Your Videos

#1) Craft a catchy benefit-rich title

Here are 2 different examples that you can use for a title. "How to Get Your Ex Back - 3 Tips for Getting Your Ex Back"

"How to Get Your Ex Back in 3 Simple Steps"

The first one title targets two keywords and the second one focuses on only one keyword but probably gets a higher click-thru

Here are 4 proven titles that you can swipe:

The 3 Most Important Things You Need to Know about ____

The 3 Best Tips on How to _____

The #1 Secret to _____

3 Tips to _____

#2) Pick an Attention-Grabbing Thumbnail

YouTube uses the exact middle frame of your video.

Consider using this knowledge to find a unique way to promote your video.

You can choose which video thumbnail to display by placing a 1 second video clip in the exact middle of the movie.

Some people put a picture of a hot girl in the thumbnail to get more clicks. While I don't personally use this technique myself, I'm sure it gets you much more views.

You don't have to sell the click with sex though. Just make sure to use some sort of interesting thumbnail that grabs people's attention or makes them curious to find what it is:

Quit Smoking
by PumpkinPigs
402,505 views

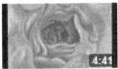
This will make you stop smoking!
by peterproscia
128,131 views

Smoking Kills (The Bryan Curtis story)
by nathpin8
371,434 views

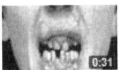
Graphic Australian Anti-Smoking Ad
by sp0ng
2,763,879 views

A very powerful ad
by Flommivids
2,509,723 views

Funny campaign against smoking
by tibilord
408,564 views

Now that you have your video optimization, it's time to focus on building backlinks!

Building Backlinks on YouTube

Most people produce a book trailer video, place it on their YouTube channel, tag it and then sit back and wait for the Mojo. Now you can do this but be prepared to wait until you fall over dead.

Once you upload your video to your YouTube Channel, tag it properly; add in your book URL and book description, you are now ready to market your book trailer.

Like backlinking, the search engines want relevant content and consistency. Your content is relevant so now let's discuss the main marketing ingredients to get traffic to your book URL on Amazon or wherever.

Video marketing is very similar to article marketing. Your video is your article and the video sharing sites are like your article submission sites.

In article marketing, if you attempt to write one article and then submit it to 200-artilce sites, the search engines simply ignore it and you receive no backlinks. They aren't stupid, people!!!

So, the smart authors go to Fiverr.com or WriteSwap.com and order 3-5 articles (or you can write them yourself) and then "spin" the articles into many multiple articles.

You can then use an article submission service and post these article to the numerous article sites and then the search engines don't ignore them because you have diversity and relevant content so now let's talk in terms of video marketing.

In video marketing, the search engines love the same three things - relevant content, diversity and consistency.

Now, like I said, you have relevant content but when it comes to diversity, you only have one video, right?

WRONG!

I am going to show you how to change your video for the search engines without changing the video...you are going to love this.

I can guarantee you that just about everybody doesn't know this technique unless you are a video engineer or video enthusiast and even then I have noticed a good many of these people are unaware that you can do this on YouTube.

It involves using the YouTube Video Editor: http://www.youtube.com/editor

Go to the editor and find one of your book trailers.

Get a list of keywords using the Google AdWords Keyword tool.

Then you "mix the video by changing the text content using one of the keywords you have selected like this:

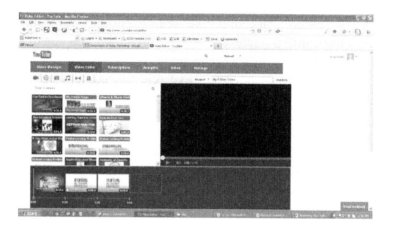

You can enlarge the screenshot for better viewing. In this case I chose my book trailer for EmbarrassingProblemsFix, which is a three part series:

Embarrassing Problems Fix - General Problems Vol 1
http://www.amazon.com/dp/B0075LOK3U
Embarrassing Problems Fix - Female Problems Vol 2
http://www.amazon.com/dp/B0075LO7AQ
Embarrassing Problems Fix - Male Problems Vol 3
http://www.amazon.com/dp/B0075LQNF8

You then click on the "a" which stands for "text" and you drag the box that says "banner" next to the trailer box like this:

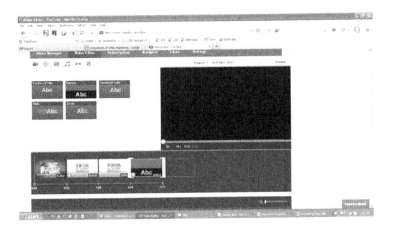

When you do this up pops a box where you can add new content and be sure the keyword you selected is included. In this case my keyword was "acne".

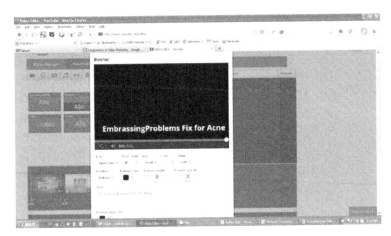

Notice that the verbiage now appears on the edited video. The search engines view this as a completely new video with new content. You can do like five of these "video mixings" per day and then sit back and watch your videos climb in the rankings.

You then submit your video to the video sharing sites...more on this in Chapter 6.

Achieving high YouTube rankings usually takes more than just good keyword optimization. How high you rank will depend on how competitive the keyword you're targeting is, as well as the number of views, likes, comments and subscribers your video has. Good "off-page optimization" on YouTube involves having lots of:

1) Views
2) Likes
3) Comments
4) Subscribers
5) Channel Views
6) Backlinks

These 6 things will lead to high rankings on YouTube, just like tons of backlinks will lead to high rankings in Google. Another perk of getting your video ranked high on YouTube is that it can get indexed right inside of Google! Now that Google owns YouTube, they typically show the 2 most popular videos in the top 5 spots. Example: How to Tie a Tie As you can see, there are 2 videos ranking #4 and #5 on Google

How would you like to have a video own 1 of those top spots? Better yet, how would you like to own two of the 2 spots with your site and a video? Dominating 2 out of the top 5 spots on Google will bring you some serious traffic! And even if you don't get the video listed in the top 5 spots, Google also feature videos at the bottom around #9 and #10 or at the top of the 2nd page too. Getting your video ranked inside of Google too without having to do any additional work is not a bad deal if you ask me. I use two additional sites to garner backlinks and both are free too:

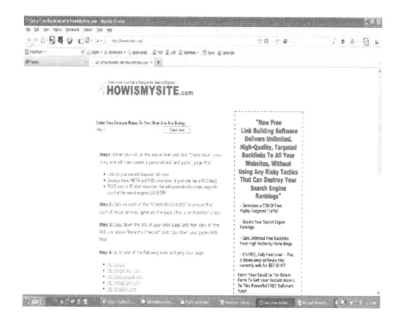

Just follow the instructions. However; be advised that you cannot use your Amazon Kindle book URL. Use your book's blog URL instead.

There are limitations but, hey…it's free!

Here is the second site and again just follow the instructions on the site.

I use Ping Farm to ping my URL:s
http://www.pingfarm.com and if you use Ping Farm they
ask for your RSS feed. If you don't have an RSS feed
then go to Feedburner.com and get a free one.

But that's not the only way Google rewards popular videos!

One of the best perks they offer is…

The YouTube Partnership Program

When you have a lot of views, likes and subscribers, you can earn "YouTube Partnership Status"

Basically, that just means that you can now make some extra money off your videos with Google Adsense.

I think most people are familiar with this by now so I'm not going to go into detail but you can make a nice chunk of change just doing this alone (not counting any of the sales you make from your videos).

I know people that are making up to 500 bucks a month just running ads on their YouTube videos. But hell, let's say you only make an extra 100 bucks a month by running ads on your videos.

That's enough to cover the cost of your hosting, your domain, your autoresponder and even outsource some SEO every month.

And if you add up 100 bucks a month for 12 months, that's over $1,200 dollars a year.

Imagine what you can do with that.

By the way, this is a very modest example as well. You can be making way more than just 100 bucks a month in Google Adsense.

Just doing this one thing alone is worth the few measly bucks you paid for this eBook. Implement it and get your money's worth!

If you want to speed up the process of getting YouTube Partnership status, the next section will reveal the factors that YouTube uses to determine your popularity. I'll also tell you the most important metric they look for in YouTube Partners (hint: it's the number of subscribers you have)

A More Detailed Look at What Determines High Rankings on YouTube

I already listed the 6 things earlier: views, likes, comments, subscribers and backlinks.

People often ask me what's "best" for getting your videos to rank high. Well, that's kind like asking what kind of SEO backlinks will get you to rank high on Google.

There's none in particular that do the trick by themselves. It's a combination of different strategies paired with good on-page optimization that leads to high rankings.

However, just like there are some backlink strategies in SEO that are worth more than others (articles vs spammy profile links) - the same goes for YouTube.

Obviously videos are one of the most important factors for ranking since that's what determines the popularity of the video.

However, I've outranked plenty of videos while having far less views than them (sometimes by as much as 20,000 less views)

One of the biggest reasons for this is optimization. That's why I spent so much time covering it in such great detail. Please do not underestimate it!

However, another one of the main reasons was how many "likes" my videos had.

I didn't discover this until after some trial and error but I found that "likes" are crucial to ranking videos high on YouTube.

What does it mean when someone likes your video?

They are indicating to YouTube (and the community as a whole) that it's quality content that they found valuable or helpful.

It's kind of like a backlink on Google.

Well, YouTube uses these user-generated indicators to determine which videos to rank at the top in order to service their community.

If you want your video to rank higher, you can get more likes to your video by clicking the link below:

http://www.youtubetrafficstorm.com/getlikes.htm

PS: if you obtain enough video likes and ratings in your video's category, you can earn YouTube honors and be featured in the top rated category for the day, week, month (or all time).

The #1 Most Important YouTube "Popularity" Factor

One of the most important factors is the amount of subscribers you have on your channel. That's why people are always trying to get people to subscribe in their videos.

The number of subscribers you have has a direct effect on the rankings of ALL the videos you have uploaded for that channel. In other words, the more subscribers your channel has, the better it is for every video uploaded to your channel.

If someone subscribes to your page, that tells YouTube that you have good content that people are willing to subscribe to and keep coming back to.

Therefore, it's in their best interest to have you rank higher because that means they'll be checking your videos and coming back to their site. That means they'll be seeing more of their ads, thus generating revenue for them.

The amount of subscribers you have plays a huge part in getting the YouTube partnership status I mentioned earlier.

If you want to speed up the process of becoming a YouTube partner so you can start running ads and generating a steady income every month with Google Adsense, you can get subscribers to your channel by clicking the link below

http://www.youtubetrafficstorm.com/getsubscribers.htm

Another perk of having a lot of subscribers is that they get notified every time you upload a new video on their home screen when they login. That makes it much more likely for you to get more views, likes and comments. Plus, when you have a lot of channel views and subscribers, you can get your actually channel to rank on YouTube too (instead of just your videos).

Because my channel is well optimized and has a ton of views and subscribers, it actually comes up on the first page of the search results for my keywords.

That means you can dominate the YouTube search engine (the 2nd most popular search engine online) and have multiple listings on the first page!

It used to be easy to do this on Google when you could easily rank articles on the first page but now it's now pretty hard to dominate 2 spots on the first page of Google.

However, it's not that hard on Youtube. There's not nearly as much competition and most people don't know how to actually get their videos to rank high on YouTube.

That's because most people on YouTube aren't internet marketers so they're not really using it strategically.

They're just doing things haphazardly and throwing stuff together hoping something sticks. They make a video, they upload and tag it with some stuff that sounds cool and that's it. They don't think about it strategically the way that I'm teaching you here. So if you apply these strategies, you'll be way ahead of the pack.

I'm not sure if you are familiar with something called "Viral Marketing" so I wanted to show you this amazing new marketing tool for video.

It's called "Staged" http://www.staged.com/ and it utilizes YouTube videos along with Facebook, Twitter, and all the other social network web sites available.

The beauty of this system is that literally everyone in the world is familiar with YouTube and has an account with a social network like Facebook. The last stat I heard was that 1 in 4 people in the world has a Facebook account!

This familiarity creates a huge level of comfort and feeling of "I can do this" here at Staged.

"Viral Marketing" is a method of marketing that basically says "Do the effort one time and watch the results continue to grow exponentially over time".

This occurs as a result of people sharing your advertisement with others. Then those people share it with people they know... and so on. Pretty soon 5-10 people who originally saw your ad can turn into hundreds or thousands of people. This is the "Viral" concept.

If you are looking for a simple way to generate traffic to any web site you own you should check this out!

Social Marker

SocialMarker.com is a free tool that allows you to submit a blog, article, video or just a link to a website or to multiple social bookmarking sites.

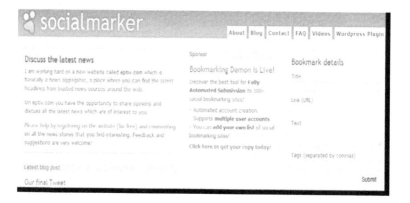

All you need to do is fill out a few form fields, hit submit and your link will be posted to all the services that you are signed up with.

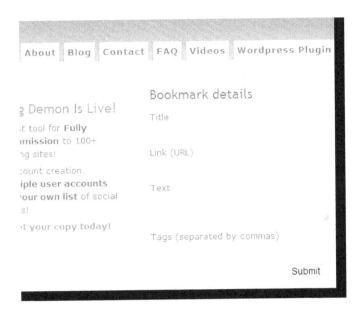

About | Blog | Contact | FAQ | Videos | Wordpress Plugin

Bookmark details

ʒ Demon Is Live!

ıt tool for **Fully**
ımission to 100+
ıg sites!

:ount creation.
iple user accounts
ıour own list of social
s!

ıt your copy today!

Title

Link (URL)

Text

Tags (separated by commas)

Submit

1. Add title

2. Add link url

3. Add description

4. Add tags

Video Sharing Sites

You can find an extensive list of video sharing sites over at Wikipedia

Notable examples

- 56.com (Chinese)
- Archive.org
- Afreeca (South Korean)
- AniBOOM
- Blinkx
- Blip.tv
- BlogTV
- Brainpop
- Break.com
- Buzznet
- Comedy.com
- Crackle
- Dailymotion
- EngageMedia
- ExpoTV
- Funnyordie.com
- Flickr
- Fotki
- Gawkk
- Hulu

- HD share * (focus on HD videos)
- Lafango
- Liveleak
- Mail.ru
- MaYoMo
- Mefeedia
- Metacafe
- Mevio
- Mobento (Focus on video search)
- Myspace
- MyVideo
- Nico Nico Douga (Japanese)
- OneWorldTV
- Openfilm
- Ourmedia
- Panopto
- Photobucket
- Podblanc
- Redtube
- Revver *
- Rambler Vision (Russian)

- ReelTime.com
- RuTube (Russian)
- Sapo Videos (Portuguese)
- SchoolTube
- ScienceStage
- Sevenload
- SmugMug
- Tangle.com (formerly Godtube)
- Trilulilu (Romanian)
- TroopTube
- Tudou (Chinese)
- Twitvid
- Vbox7 (Bulgarian)
- Veoh
- Viddler
- Videojug
- Videolog (Portuguese)
- Vidoosh (Iranian)

- Vidyard
- Vimeo
- Vuze
- Vzaar
- Wildscreen tv
- Wistia
- Yahoo! Video
- Youku (Chinese)
- YouTube
- Zoopy

Tube Mogul

TubeMogul is the only video marketing company built for branding. TubeMogul integrates real-time media buying, ad serving, targeting, optimization and brand measurement. You can register for free and can upload to 5 different video sharing sites.

TubeMogul use to be just a video sharing site. Now they are a full-blown sharing, analytics and video marketing behemoth. Go here for the sharing site:

http://www.oneload.com/

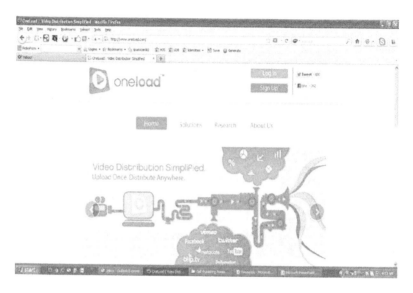

Here is their analytics site: http://videohub.tv/

Video Optimizing Checklist

How to Optimize Your Videos to Rank High on YouTube

1) What's the keyword you're trying to rank with this video for?

2) Is the keyword you want to rank in the video title?

3) Is your keyword in the tags, along with any other related keywords that you want to rank?

4) Is your URL the first thing in the description box and is it actually clickable?
If it's not the first thing in the box, people won't see it and if there's no http in front of it won't be clickable.

Use   this   format   =>
http://www.YourWebsiteHere.com

5) Are your main keywords used in the description box below the URL and call to action? This is what a well optimized video should look like.

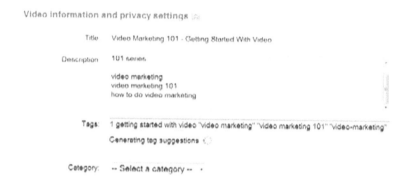

Here are 3 main keywords this video is trying to rank:

"Video Marketing" "Video Marketing 101" "Getting Started with Video

As you can see, they are all in the title box, the description box and the tag box (though you don't see them all in the tags in this screenshot)
Here are some more general guidelines to follow:

☐ Only focus on 1 or 2 keywords per video and don't try to rank a video for more than 2 or 3 keywords.

It's better to narrow in on one or two keywords and be perfectly optimized for them than it is to try to rank 3-4 different keywords with 1 video and miss them all because you were trying to hit them all with 1 swing.

☐ Always make sure you put the full title in the tags and each of the individual keywords as well.

☐ Put your keywords in quotes in the tags, it helps.

☐ Put your keywords in the description box too.

The Optimization "Short-Cut"

1) Find the top 5 videos in your niche or for your keyword
2) Pull up their video and look at their tags
3) Copy and paste the tags they're using into your tags

This will help you rank on YouTube for the same keywords they're targeting and it'll also get your video featured on the sidebar where it shows the related videos.

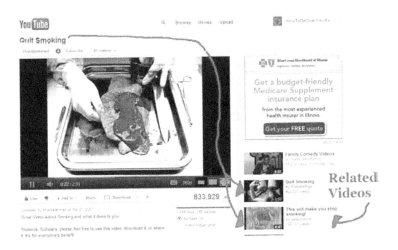

What YouTube does is it "sniffs out" related videos based on the keyword relevancy in the titles, tags, and description etc.

So if you're optimized the same as the most popular videos, you have a much better chance of having your video featured to the right. It's basically like having PPC/Banner Ads featured on the sidebar of one the most popular websites in your niche.

Except it's totally free!

This is probably my favorite part about YouTube.

If you tag your videos right, they basically do the promotion FOR you. They feature your videos on the sidebar of other related videos and you get tons of views from people that are clicking around on all the related videos and watching video after video.

I don't know about you but I'm kind of lazy so the idea of optimizing my video correctly and getting views right away without having to build any links is pretty sweet. That'll never happen with SEO.

Chapter 4 – What Books Make the Best Videobooks

Video

This is important. Not every genre can use the videobook format. I created a rather lengthy list (138 pages) of categories that I found on Amazon.com.

Most of the books that I review are wrongly categorized in the KDP platform.

Remember categories are one of the six searchable fields that the search engines index so this is very important. Go here to get the list:

http://www.filefactory.com/f/fe82c7e529c85112

To determine what categories on the list can be made into videobooks, ask yourself if it is a category that you would buy a videobook for.

Example: a genre such as single-recipe cookbooks would NOT be a good choice. Remember, although a book may qualify to be made into a videobook, make sure it is a topic and genre that sells. This is important! Children's books sell well as videobooks because kids can interact with them as the storyline is read and keeps them entertained in the car or vat home so mom can get other things done. Bear this in mind, the best videobooks entertain and educate.

The best genres are children's books, travel books, pictorial books, novels of any kind such as westerns, any kind of "Advice & How To" books including training books and instruction manuals of any type.

As a bonus, I also placed my videobook PowerPoint template that I use to place my content and illustrations correctly in the same download portal as the Amazon Categories above. If you use it too then you won't be making the silly mistakes that I did.

Chapter 5 – Illustrating Your Book for Video

I have already turned you on to my graphics lady who does my work and again she rocks! Before you engage her on Skype or email, think about what needs to be done.

Every PowerPoint frame should have an illustration that is part of the storyline being narrated in that frame.

Using the template I gave you in the last chapter; lay out your book in each slide so that any graphic designer can match the illustration to the dialogue.

What I am referring to as illustrations are graphically designed drawings. In lieu of this, you can use photos, pictures, artwork, or anything visual that matches the narrative dialogue being spoken.

See my example illustrations below…

These are from the book, "The Power of Trained Observation" and the book is a course that teaches observation training. Notice that in lieu of drawing illustrations, photos and pics were used. In the resource section, I have given numerous sites to get royalty-free pics.

•Psychology only studies the observable aspects of the mind and discounts the unseen or intangible aspects of the human mind.

•Behavioral science attempts to study the intangible aspects of the human mind...why you do the things you do and more importantly why you don't do what you should do.

•There is no such thing as commercial psychology versus personal psychology. The mind uses the same mechanism to evaluate all types of relationships.

•Everything we do revolves around relationships. We relate to our environment, our friends, family, co-workers, other people and even our pets. We are social animals.

Building Relationships

ForensicsNation

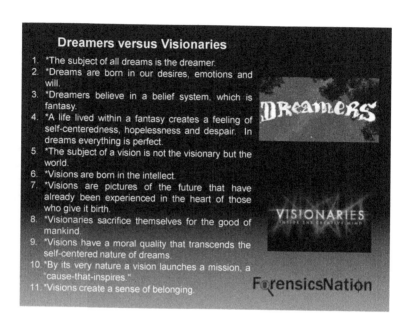

Dreamers versus Visionaries

1. *The subject of all dreams is the dreamer.
2. *Dreams are born in our desires, emotions and will.
3. *Dreamers believe in a belief system, which is fantasy.
4. *A life lived within a fantasy creates a feeling of self-centeredness, hopelessness and despair. In dreams everything is perfect.
5. *The subject of a vision is not the visionary but the world.
6. *Visions are born in the intellect.
7. *Visions are pictures of the future that have already been experienced in the heart of those who give it birth.
8. *Visionaries sacrifice themselves for the good of mankind.
9. *Visions have a moral quality that transcends the self-centered nature of dreams.
10. *By its very nature a vision launches a mission, a "cause-that-inspires."
11. *Visions create a sense of belonging.

DREAMERS

VISIONARIES

ForensicsNation

Okay, let's move on to the resource section now...

Chapter 6 – Videobook Resources

Graphic Designer
Sanchita Dutta
solution.bn@gmail.com
www.bnsolution.in

Author's Note: I use Sanchita for all of my graphic needs. In my opinion, she is the best and her prices cannot be beat. Sanchita is also a HTML coding expert and a Wordpress expert. I am very hard pressed to finds something she cannot do. She is an expert animator and has produced some stunning work for me such as below:

Videobook Producer
Subject TV
Daniel Chapnick

dchapnick@subjecttv.com

Author's Note: Daniel Chapnick is an excellent resource to produce your videobook. He has a bevy of narrators that he uses and a full video production house.

Free Camtasia Studio
http://www.techsmith.com/download/camtasiatrial.asp
Key: HCABK-2QTCC-M9P59-ET4HX-F4D93

Free Recording Software
http://audacity.sourceforge.net/

Image Marketing Sites (Free Rights)
http://www.public-domain-photos.com/
http://imagebase.davidniblack.com/
http://www.freephotosbank.com/
http://www.freejpg.com.ar/
http://www.cepolina.com/freephoto/
http://visipix.dynalia3.com/index_hidden.htm
http://www.burningwell.org/gallery2/main.php
http://tofz.org/
http://stock.diwiesign.com/
http://www.unprofound.com/
http://www.freefoto.com/
http://amygdela.com/stock/
http://www.zurb.net/zurbphotos/
http://energy.star29.net/store/
http://www.photogen.com/
http://www.freedigitalphotos.net/
http://www.sxc.hu
http://www.dreamstime.com/free-photos
http://office.microsoft.com/en-us/images

http://www.kozzi.com
http://www.morguefile.com/
http://freerangestock.com
http://www.rgbstock.com/

Music
www.PumpAudio.com
http://www.acidplanet.com
http://www.royaltyfreemusic.com
http://www.wavtracks.com
http://www.premiumbeat.com
http://www.ibaudio.com
http://www.musicbakery.com

Miscellaneous
http://www.techsmith.com/snagit-upgrade.html
http://www.staged.com/
http://goanimate.com/
https://gumroad.com/
http://www.videolaunch.net/
http://www.tubemogul.com/
http://www.oneload.com/
http://springrank.com/
http://tremorvideo.com/
http://www.sparkol.com/home
http://www.grammarly.com/
http://paperrater.com/
http://www.flipsnack.com/
http://www.storytellingmachines.com/

Photography
http://www.gettyimages.com/?country=usa
http://www.istockphoto.com/index.php

http://www.istockphoto.com/video
http://www.jupitermedia.com/
http://photobucket.com/
http://www.wireimage.com/

Pics-Photo
http://www.picturetrail.com/photoFlick/samples/acrobatcube/l_acrobatcube.shtml
http://www.sliderocket.com/
http://rockyou.com/ry/home
http://www.slide.com/
http://www.photographersindex.com/
http://www.picresize.com/
http://mypictr.com/
http://snipshot.com/

Public Domain Sites
http://www.abebooks.com/
http://www.alibris.com/
http://www.bartleby.com/
http://buyoutfootage.com/
http://www.gutenberg.org/wiki/Main_Page
http://www.filmchest.com/
http://emol.org/movies/
http://www.ibiblio.org/

http://www.archive.org/details/movies
http://www.oclc.org/us/en/global/default.htm
http://www.publicdomaintorrents.net/
http://www.kickbuttideas.com/pd/
http://www.readprint.com/

Video Sharing Sites

http://www.ebaumsworld.com/
http://www.spike.com/
http://break.com/
http://www.metacafe.com/
http://www.atom.com/
http://www.veoh.com/home.html
http://vodpod.com/tag/grouper
http://www.Dailymotion.com
http://www.Blip.tv
http://www.screencast.com/
http://wooshii.com/
http://www.zillatube.com./
http://www.slideshare.net/
http://www.screenr.com/
http://robo.to/
http://www.flixya.com
http://www.uvouch.com
http://www.magnify.net/sites/categories
http://www.ulinkx.com/
http://www.myvidster.com
http://www.gemzies.com/
http://www.infectiousvideos.com/
http://www.videosift.com
http://www.vewgle.com
http://www.tagged.com
http://www.wonderhowto.com
http://http://www.maxior.pl
http://www.nowpublic.com
http://www.vodpod.com
http://www.kontraband.com
http://www.ttr2.co.uk
http://www.flabber.nl
http://www.abum.com

http://www.voomed.com
http://www.beautyandthedirt.com
http://www.boredjunk.com
http://www.directgamez.com
http://www.myarcadespot.com
http://www.godofhumor.com
http://www.prankies.com
http://www.jabers.com
www.ridiculousvideos.com
http://www.dumbr.com
http://www.pan-fun.com
http://www.shockthis.com
http://www.exbyte.net
http://www.vidaxs.com
http://www.boredtown.com
www.milkandcookies.com
http://www.theaffiliated.net/
http://www.boxee.tv/
http://www.brightroll.com/
http://www.dailymotion.com/us
http://www.desksite.net/
http://www.hulu.com/
http://www.mefeedia.com/
http://www.red-lever.com/
http://www.revver.com/
http://www.scanscout.com/
http://eyespot.com/
http://crackle.com/
http://jumpcut.com/
http://ourmedia.org/
http://vimeo.com/
http://www.vsocial.com/
http://www.tremormedia.com

http://www.vibrantmedia.com/
http://www.vidcat.com/
http://www.videoegg.com/
http://www.vidsense.com/
http://vlaze.com/
http://www.volomedia.com/
http://www.yumenetworks.com
http://video.yahoo.com/
http://vids.myspace.com/
http://video.msn.com
http://video.aol.com/
http://www.heavy.com/
http://video.google.com/
http://www.tubemogul.com
http://www.youtube.com/
http://imageshack.us/
http://yfrog.com/
http://www.viddler.com
http://www.adhysteria.com
http://www.bofunk.com
http://www.esnips.com
http://www.guba.com
http://www.iviewtube.com
http://www.kewega.com
http://www.livevideo.com
http://www.megavideo.com
http://www.motionbox.com
http://www.photobucket.com
http://www.sharkle.com
http://www.u2upfly.com
http://www.vidilife.com
http://www.viddyou.com
http://www.screencast.com/pricing.aspx

Video Embedding Sites
http://www.WonderHowTo.com
http://www.flixya.com
http://www.spike.com
http://www.instructables.com
http://www.myspace.com
http://www.uvouch.com
http://www.magnify.net/sites/categories
http://www.ulinkx.com/
http://www.gemzies.com/
http://www.infectiousvideos.com/
http://www.videosift.com
http://www.vewgle.com
http://www.tagged.com
http://www.wonderhowto.com
http://http://www.maxior.pl
http://www.nowpublic.com
http://www.myvidster.com
http://www.ning.com
http://www.vodpod.com
http://www.mefeedia.com

Voice Overs
http://www.voices.com/
http://VoiceTalentNow.com
http://www.provoiceusa.com
http://amazingvoicetalent.com
http://www.provoiceusa.com

I Have a Special Gift for My Readers

I appreciate my readers for without them I am just another author attempting to make a difference. If my book has made a favorable impression please leave me an honest review. Thank you in advance for you participation.

My readers and I have in common a passion for the written word as well as the desire to learn and grow from books.

My special offer to you is a massive ebook library that I have compiled over the years. It contains hundreds of fiction and non-fiction ebooks in Adobe Acrobat PDF format as well as the Greek classics and old literary classics too.

In fact, this library is so massive to completely download the entire library will require over 5 GBs open on your desktop.

Use the link below and scan all of the ebooks in the library. You can select the ebooks you want individually or download the entire library.

The link below does not expire after a given time period so you are free to return for more books rather than clog your desktop. And feel free to give the link to your friends who enjoy reading too.

I thank you for reading my book and hope if you are pleased that you will leave me an honest review so that I can improve my work and or write books that appeal to your interests.

Okay, here is the link…

http://tinyurl.com/special-readers-promo

PS: If you wish to reach me personally for any reason you may simply write to mailto:support@epubwealth.com.

I answer all of my emails so rest assured I will respond.

Meet the Author

Dr. Treat Preston is a behavioral scientist specializing in all types of relationships and associated problems, psychological triggers as applied to commercial advertising and marketing, and energy psychology. He is a best-selling author with numerous books dealing on publishing, behavioral science, marketing and more. He is also one of the lead research scientists with AppliedMindSciences.com, the mind research unit of ForensicsNation.com.

He and his wife Cynthia reside in Auburn, California.

Visit some of his websites

http://www.AddMeInNow.com
http://www.AppliedMindSciences.com
http://www.BookbuilderPLUS.com
http://www.BookJumping.com
http://www.EmailNations.com
http://www.EmbarrassingProblemsFix.com
http://www.ePubWealth.com
http://www.ForensicsNation.com
http://www.ForensicsNationStore.com
http://www.FreebiesNation.com
http://www.HealthFitnessWellnessNation.com
http://www.Neternatives.com
http://www.PrivacyNations.com
http://www.RetireWithoutMoney.org
http://www.SurvivalNations.com
http://www.TheBentonKitchen.com
http://www.Theolegions.org
http://www.VideoBookbuilder.com

Made in the USA
Middletown, DE
11 May 2023

30346962R00046